The Waiting Season

What to Do When God Has You in a Holding Pattern

Erick W. Hoskin

Sermon To Book
www.sermontobook.com

The Waiting Season / Erick W. Hoskin
ISBN-13: 978-1-945793-78-3
ISBN-10: 1-945793-78-3

To my family, for believing in me and seeing the greatness in me when I didn't even know it existed. Because of your love and support, I dedicate this book to you!

CONTENTS

Waiting Is Preparation

There is one thought on your mind as you pack your clothes into the suitcase—to get back to your family. Your work is finished, and you long to see the ones you love. Leaving them was difficult, and the difficulty increased with every minute of separation. The flight home is scheduled to leave in a few hours. Soon you will be on your way to easing the longing in your heart.

Flying is easy, fast, and efficient compared to traveling from state to state in a SUV, but you still have to do a lot of waiting. Once you load your bags into the shuttle, you have to wait to get to the airport. Then you wait in line at the ticket counter. You wait to pass through security, you wait to board, you wait for takeoff, you wait during the flight, you wait in an unexpected and frustrating holding pattern over your city, and you wait for the plane to unload. All of this must happen before you are finally reunited with your family.

While you waited for the desire of your heart to be fulfilled, what were you doing? What did your longing to be with your family lead you to reflect on? Even though your desire wasn't immediately satisfied, the waiting wasn't wasted. You prepared your heart for seeing your family. You imagined what it would be like to walk through the halls of your house again, to sleep in your own bed, and to have a face-to-face conversation with those you love.

Our lives are filled with seasons, and like seasons of the earth, the seasons of our lives change. Sometimes we bask in summer sun and joy. Other times, we suffer the pain, loss, and scarcity of winter. Sometimes budding life offers new, exciting opportunities and challenges.

Waiting is a season every Christian will experience. However, you need to understand that your waiting season is not a wasted season. Whether that season is as brief as a flight from city to city or it is a longer period of waiting for something God has put on your heart to come to fruition, what you may think of as a waiting season is God's preparation season.

Are you waiting for a better job or to finish school? Are you waiting to hear from the doctor about tests? Are you waiting for a relationship to cool or to heat up? Are you waiting for God to change something in your frustrating life? We're all going somewhere. We're all in a season of waiting for something.

Since God is Alpha and Omega and He already knows your beginning from your ending, you can trust that He is preparing you for your future as well as choreographing your future for you. He is also working on the hearts of people He will use to bless you in your next season. God, the master architect, is strategically accomplishing growth in you to meet the needs of those you'll come across in the future, people you don't even know yet.

Proverbs 3:5–6 says, "Trust in the LORD with all your heart and lean not on your own understanding; in all your ways submit to him, and he will make your paths straight." If you're in a waiting season, God is preparing you for where you're going.

Knowing that He is preparing you doesn't necessarily make the waiting easy. Waiting is one of life's most difficult tasks. However, you can learn how to grow patiently in grace. You can understand that God's timing is always perfect. Waiting seasons aren't wasted seasons. They're seasons of growing into the person God wants you to be.

If you now understand that you have a destination for your life that is greater than where you are, you must ask yourself whether you are prepared for where you are going. The delay you may experience is God's ordained season of pause to develop your capacity to handle what He has in store for you. He will stretch your faith to the point where you depend on Him alone.

In that faith-stretching process, God will compel you to dispose of unwanted baggage you have convinced yourself you need for where you are going. He knows that if you try to carry the extra weight to your destination, you will compromise His greater purpose. Why go to your season of blessing wearing the same mentality from which God is trying to deliver you? God knows what you need for where you are going.

God will use your waiting time to take you from

unprepared to fully prepared in Him. You may feel prepared, but only God knows what lies ahead. Only He can prepare you for the rigors, trials, and burdens in your future, as well as develop your capacity to enjoy His benefits. Even if you already feel prepared, you can trust that the time of waiting has a purpose, His purpose.

Are you in a waiting season? Are you circling in a holding pattern over the city before you can fulfill the longing God has given you? You're living in the most exciting time God has to offer, a time of growth and fulfillment. He is directing your paths. Do you trust Him?

To find out what God means for you to do during a waiting season, read on. You'll learn why you can't stay where you are, how to shed extra baggage, and why you should trust that God's delivery of blessings is right on schedule. You'll also discover what a new man looks like and the importance of keeping your eye on the prize. At the end of each chapter, a workbook section will help you examine your life and put the lessons into action.

If you're not sure how these ideas apply to your waiting season, turn the page to see how you can take full advantage of this indispensable time God has given you.

CHAPTER ONE

You Can't Stay Here

Abram lived well. Genesis 11 and 12 describe a man of wealth with excellent business skills and a family man who was loved. What more could he possibly need? Other than a son to carry on his name and wealth, there wasn't much more he needed to make a comfortable life. He was in a season of blessing.

So why did he pack up, risk his wealth, and venture into a season of waiting? He received a powerful message, and he chose to believe and be faithful.

> The LORD had said to Abram, "Go from your country, your people and your father's household to the land I will show you."
> —Genesis 12:1

How did Abram know what the future held? The command came with a promise, a longing that would be fulfilled if he did as God commanded:

"I will make you into a great nation, and I will bless you; I will make your name great, and you will be a blessing. I will bless those who bless you, and whoever curses you I will curse; and all peoples on earth will be blessed through you."

—Genesis 12:2–3

God promised to make from Abram a great nation, which meant that he and his wife, Sarai, would have the child they wanted. Abram's name, soon to be changed to Abraham, would be great.

He was confronted with a command and a promise, but he surely saw the season of uncertainty ahead. In Abram's day, the challenges of moving weren't simply packing all of one's possessions in a truck, finding a new house, and starting a new job. The risks Abram was taking were mind-boggling. He and those traveling with him could be attacked on the way and slaughtered. If they didn't find grass for the herds, they would lose everything. If they didn't come across water or wells, they would die. What if they didn't find empty land where they could settle? That could mean war.

What did Abram do?

So Abram went, as the LORD had told him; and Lot went with him. Abram was seventy-five years old when he set out from Harran. He took his wife Sarai, his nephew Lot, all the possessions they had accumulated and the people they had acquired in Harran, and they set out for the land of Canaan, and they arrived there.

Abram traveled through the land as far as the site of the

great tree of Moreh at Shechem. At that time the Canaanites were in the land. The LORD appeared to Abram and said, "To your offspring I will give this land." So he built an altar there to the LORD, who had appeared to him.
—Genesis 12:4–7

Abram continued on, traveling in faith, unable to conceive how he would be the father of a great nation. Abram was on a journey to becoming Abraham. He was the same man who would receive the covenant from God detailed in Genesis 17, but he was not ready yet. He needed to become someone new.

Many of us have no idea what our names shall be or the magnitude of the blessing that is in our future. The crushing you are enduring in your season of becoming is a necessary part of God's plan for where you are going. You must trust the process. Between Genesis 12 and Genesis 17, we see that Abram had a calling season, a testing season, and an obedience season. Through all of this, he became Abraham.

Abraham had to trust the process and go through the developmental stages to get where he needed to be. I'm certain that he had questions and doubts. He was a man who often succumbed to fear of the unknown. Sometimes he failed. But ultimately, despite his shortcomings, he is remembered and recorded as a man who "against all hope, … in hope believed and so became the father of many nations, just as it had been said to him" (Romans 4:18).

Abram's Failure and God's Forgiveness

When Abram arrived in the Negev and settled down,

famine struck the land. Instead of trusting that God would care for him and his household, he decided to travel to Egypt.

Abram's wife, Sarai, was beautiful, and Abram was nervous.

> As he was about to enter Egypt, he said to his wife Sarai, "I know what a beautiful woman you are. When the Egyptians see you, they will say, 'This is his wife.' Then they will kill me but will let you live. Say you are my sister, so that I will be treated well for your sake and my life will be spared because of you."
> —*Genesis 12:11–13*

Sarai followed her husband's plan (Genesis 12:10–20; 13:1–2). When the Egyptians noticed how beautiful she was, they took her to Pharaoh, bringing Abram with them. Abram was treated well. He was given cattle, camels, donkeys, sheep, and servants. However, disease spread through Pharaoh's house, and Pharaoh discovered that Sarai was Abram's wife. In his anger at the deception, Pharaoh kicked Abram out of the country. As Abram returned to the Negev, where he should have stayed to begin with, God blessed him.

If God has His hands on you, you have an anointing like Abram had. If only you knew the power of God that is on your life and how unstoppable you are, nothing could hinder the plan God has for you. You don't have to lie or scheme to protect His anointing. The anointing on your life attracts the blessings and favor of God.

Abram's fear kept him from staying in the waiting

season. His anointing didn't happen after the season, but before. Abram's waiting season in the Negev was anointed by God and protected by God for his growth, but Abram feared the famine and the Egyptians and doubted God's faithfulness. You must remember to trust in God's anointing so you can stay on track during your waiting season.

Trusting God to Grow What's Inside of You

What you will become is already inside of you. Growing in faith and trusting the process, however, is difficult. That faith comes from putting your confidence in God. This confidence does not come from trust in yourself. It's not a trust in things. It is trust in God—His goodness, faithfulness, and efficacy.

This harkens back to Proverbs 3:5–6: "Trust in the LORD with all your heart and lean not on your own understanding; in all your ways submit to him, and he will make your paths straight." Don't trust fact or feeling. Instead, have faith in Christ Jesus. Consult with Him in prayer, read His Word, and watch your ways as you enter the season of waiting.

Confidence in God is not confidence in other people. We often walk side by side with other believers, and sometimes we create codependency with other people.

I'll always remember the time when God broke the codependency I had developed with my parents. Parents can become enablers of their adult child if they establish themselves as their kid's safety net. Anytime I would fall short of being able to pay my monthly bills, I knew that I could call on my parents and they would send me some money.

I'll never forget the day that arrangement came to an end. I was a young newly-wed. I had the mounting pressure of providing for a family, but I did not have the money to take care of some of my household responsibilities. I remember calling my mother on the phone and giving her my sob story about how I needed a few extra dollars to pay some bills for the month. And my mother said no.

She said, "Son, it's not that I don't have the money to send. But this is a time when you need to learn to trust God. Have you prayed about it?" I hadn't. Then she said, "Why don't you pray to God about it first? Trust Him with all of your heart."

We did make it through that tough season, but the lesson my mother gave me was even more important. I now understand the importance of praying to God about everything. Talk to Him first, and He will work everything out for your good.

Trust that God is growing what's inside of you. Break from the codependency and become dependent on God, and you'll find that your confidence comes from Him and nowhere else! When you find your confidence in God, you will be positioned to receive His blessings and to become who He created you to be.

When our trust is in God, it attracts God's favor. God showers His children with blessings in order to reveal His love and also as motivation for us to continue in faith and obedience.

When I refer to God's blessings, I don't mean merely

the material blessings of this world. In fact, we don't need God for material things. However, there may be times in our lives when we see the hand of God bless us with things we can't afford. We may see God open doors and bless us with promotions for which our degrees don't qualify us.

Our focus should be on using our waiting season to develop the capacity to handle what God has for us. Otherwise, we could be the hindrance that halts us from receiving our blessings from God.

What's Blocking the Blessings?

God will develop you in your waiting season so that you can become what He has called you to be in your due season. Too often we feel that we are ready for our due season when we haven't even allowed God's Word to shape us and make us ready.

Roadblocks to Blessings

Here's a short list of issues that can cause us to stumble during our time of waiting:

- We want promotion without the pressure.
- We want perfection without the process.
- We want one step from the starting line to the finish line.
- We want to know the end of the story.
- We aren't willing to depart from the comfy

confines of our human-made reality and take a leap of faith into the unknown.

- We think that life is a race to acquire things, rather than a journey into the divine.

Where you are is not necessarily a bad place, but it's not where your blessing is or where God wants you to end up. Your development in the becoming season God has ordained for you starts with your walk of faith. That's where the blessings begin. The blessing God has with your name on it is wrapped up in the obedience of your departure.

We often want to jump into our due season before we've gone through our becoming season. Wait. Be patient, but don't get too comfortable. Like Abraham, you have to get up and go. You need to follow God in faith, not giving in to fear. God has blessings for you as you obey His call. He is not going to bless you unless you follow His command.

Don't let your circle become your grave. Sometimes in order to find out who you are, you have to get away from the people, places, and things you know.

Consider what happened with Abram's father:

Terah took his son Abram, his grandson Lot son of Haran, and his daughter-in-law Sarai, the wife of his son Abram, and together they set out from Ur of the Chaldeans to go to Canaan. But when they came to Harran, they settled there.

Terah lived 205 years, and he died in Harran.
—Genesis 11:31–32

Perhaps Terah intended to go to the land God would promise to the descendants of Abraham, but he stopped in Harran and eventually died there. It was then that God gave Abram His promise and His call. Abram and his father started out together, but God already had a plan for Abram's life.

It's possible that you may not receive your Genesis 12 instructions until your "Terah" dies. Moving forward may involve letting go of some things. For example, perhaps you are called to serve in the church, but you don't have time because you're working multiple jobs. Perhaps it's time to get serious about stewardship and budgeting and trusting God so you can follow Him into service. Maybe you have a group of friends who like to gossip all of the time, and you need to let your association with them die so you can find another group of friends who uplift each other in the Lord.

What's stopping you from hearing your instructions from God? What do you need to let die? As painful as these changes can be, when you look back over your life, you can see that had some people not left you, had the boss not fired you, had some doors not closed in your face, you would not have been positioned to become who you are becoming.

The time of becoming can be a lonely time. This is a season when it's all about your faith in God. You won't necessarily get confirmation from those close to you. They may not understand the assignment or your decision to obey God's instructions. They may see you change and pull away or even accuse you of acting funny, but you're not in your season to win the approval of other people. It's about you and God working together. Make sure you're listening to God first and obeying without stopping.

Another block to finding His blessings is waiting for perfection in yourself. Notice that God didn't speak to Abraham; He gave the assignment to Abram. God doesn't wait to call us until we become who He wants us to be. He calls us in our imperfection, before we start becoming, so that we can do His perfect will. Waiting until you're perfect isn't a good option because no one, except Christ, will ever be perfect. Don't use your imperfection as an excuse to keep you from doing what God has called you to do.

Abraham wouldn't have become the father of many nations if he had not left the comforts of the familiar. What major blessings are you delaying by playing it safe and walking by sight instead of by faith (2 Corinthians 5:7)?

Sometimes relationships and connections have to end before we can step into God's will and our season of waiting and growth. God told Abraham to leave the land. He also told him to leave the people he knew. This included Lot. However, as you may have noticed in our reading at the beginning of the chapter, Lot joined him. In the next chapter, we'll discuss how we can cause problems when we don't follow God's call completely.

Full obedience in our season of becoming is a journey of faith and blessings. What's holding you back?

WORKBOOK

Chapter One Questions

Question: What vision or burden has God given you for your life? What fears do you have about His plans?

_____

_____

_____

_____

_____

_____

_____

_____

_____

_____

_____

Question: Describe a time when hardship caused you to doubt or run from God's plan. How did stepping away from His will lead to greater complications or a loss of blessings in your life?

_____

_____

_____

_____

_____

_____

_____

_____

_____

_____

_____

_____

Question: Review the list of things that block God's blessings. Are any of these true in your own life? How can learning to wait on God eliminate the blessing blockers?

_____

_____

_____

_____

_____

_____

_____

_____

_____

_____

_____

_____

Action: Divide a paper into two columns. Label one side "Self-Confidence" and the other side "Confidence in God." Now contrast these two ideas. How can you tell which one supplies your underlying motivation?

Chapter One Notes

_____

_____

_____

_____

_____

_____

_____

_____

_____

_____

_____

_____

_____

_____

_____

_____

_____

_____

_____

_____

_____

CHAPTER TWO

Releasing Those People God Has Released

Has God ever spoken to you vividly about something you needed? He has to me.

My ministry took me to San Francisco, California. I had to fly there and back. It wasn't going to be a long trip, and I should have packed light. Everyone else in the world would have packed a simple bag with a few changes of clothes and some toiletry essentials.

Not me.

Somehow I ended up packing everything in my closet. Yes, everything I owned—all of my clothes, shoes, and belts, plus extra books and chargers for phones I used to have. Everything. I wouldn't use ten percent of what I brought. I was carrying extra bags I wouldn't even unzip on the trip.

God had worked it so that my sister would be traveling to Houston while I was in San Francisco. She sent me a picture of herself at the airport, along with a message that she was traveling light for the week. Beside her was her only bag, a carry-on.

I glanced down at what would have been the bedroom floor if it hadn't been covered with my bags. Did I really need all of this for just three days away from home?

When I arrived at the check-in counter, the attendant asked me to place my suitcase onto the scale. I watched the number shoot past fifty pounds, the airline's weight limit for a bag. The woman was kind as she explained the bad news. I would need to pay $70, or I could buy another bag for $50. I opted to save the $20. In moments, my bags were strewn across the airport's tiled floor, and people were watching me dig through a month's worth of clothing changes.

I learned two important lessons that day. First of all, my sister was onto something. Carrying too much weight made me spend far more energy, money, and mental concern than I should have. I needed to shed some of that weight. The second thing I learned was that I wanted to bring too much. I had to carry additional bags because I couldn't part from what I thought I needed.

Leaving Things Behind

Abram, whose name means "exalted father," was informed by God that there were great things ahead.[1] He would need to enter a new season, but he would become so much more than he already was.

God shared with Abram that there were three difficult things he would have to do in order to go to the next level. If he did these things, God would bless him. God instructed Abram to leave his country, his family, and his father's house. We saw in the last chapter that he left, but the leaving was harder than we initially discussed. Terah, Abram's father, had died (Genesis 11:32). Abram was positioned to take over the massive household. He was rich and powerful and held plenty of land. When God commanded Abram to leave, it meant that he would be leaving behind his dwellings, the enormous clan and family, and his father's house, where he had responsibility and leadership. The others looked to him for wisdom and guidance. He provided stability in the region. God asked him to leave all of this.

The pressure to stay was powerful. Not only was it risky to travel into unknown territory, but Abram would also be destabilizing the region. These intense demands from God—to leave his home, his clan, and his family in a world where this was not typical—could bring ruin if God were not holding a sovereign hand over Abram. The level of faith needed to follow through was nothing short of impossible. Even the blessings God promised to Abram in Genesis 12:2–3 seemed impossible since Abram had no son to carry on his name and become a great nation.

Let's look more closely at the details of God's command to Abram.

The LORD had said to Abram, "Go from your country, your people and your father's household to the land I will show you."
—Genesis 12:1

Abram was to leave the land where he was living and

his father's household and travel to a new land.

So Abram went, as the LORD had told him; and Lot went with him. Abram was seventy-five years old when he set out from Harran. He took his wife Sarai, his nephew Lot, all the possessions they had accumulated and the people they had acquired in Harran, and they set out for the land of Canaan, and they arrived there.
—Genesis 12:4–5

Why did Lot, Abram's nephew, go on the journey? Abram wasn't supposed to take him. After Abram found some trouble in Egypt, as we discussed in the previous chapter, Lot started to make trouble. Abram was forced to "play God" in Lot's life, instead of pointing Lot to God. Abram's blessings hinged on obedience to God, something Lot didn't understand.

When God blessed Abram with livestock, silver, and gold, Lot reaped the rewards, too (Genesis 13:1–5). But was he grateful? Hardly. Lot's and Abram's herders quarreled over grazing and watering rights (Genesis 13:6–7). When Abram and Lot decided to go in different directions, who had the first choice? Lot did (Genesis 13:8–12).

Then Lot fell into the wicked ways of the evil city of Sodom. Not once, but twice, Abram came to Lot's rescue: first from invaders, then from the destruction God brought upon Sodom for its wickedness (Genesis 14:11–24; Genesis 18:16–19:29). After all of the trouble Lot caused his Uncle Abram, don't you wonder if Abram regretted having brought Lot along? Lot was a huge burden. Lot was someone Abram had been commanded to leave behind. While we don't know for sure, isn't it possible that Lot also might have found less trouble if he had stayed in Harran?

When God presents us with our calling, we all have "Lots"—people and things that will hinder us—that we need to leave behind.

Shedding the Baggage

God has a purpose for each and every one of us. You have a destiny, a divine destination toward which God is leading you, but how and when you get there depends on your faith and your obedience to His will for your life. Once you accept your calling and begin to walk toward your destiny, God will strategically force you to get rid of things and people that cannot fit where you are going.

These things will grow obvious as you proceed, but sometimes the waiting season takes time. Because He knows the plan for your life, God will allow you to sit in a divine holding pattern orchestrated to force you to shed some weight while you wait.

Many times, as in Abram's life, Satan's strategy is to bombard you with so much stuff, so many distractions, that you are not able to focus on getting into the Word as God commanded (Joshua 1:8). You're too busy with worldly concerns to attend church, develop your relationship with God, and make progress toward your destiny.

A lot of the stress you are dealing with is a result of trying to resolve conflicts with baggage you should never have brought with you on your journey. If you had left behind the extra weight where it belonged, you would have been spared some of the headaches and heartaches you are experiencing.

Perhaps most of your prayer time is dedicated to some-one you should have left behind. You didn't have the spiritual fortitude to go through with the full instructions of God, and now you're paying a price in your waiting season. You're not able to focus on your becoming sea-son. This distraction is causing you to postpone your arrival at your destiny.

If you dissect most of your stress and you find that it's because of a single person or group of people, it's time to cut those ties. Are you trying to resolve the madness in other people's lives? Maybe God has them in a trial sea-son and you're not meant to take on those trials for them. Are you giving them room in your luggage even though they don't belong there, like that extra pair of pants I should have kept out of my bag? Are you holding on to grudges or bitterness that are weighing you down like bags of rocks? Are you being generous and vulnerable in a way that becomes an obstacle?

It is okay to strive for the next level for yourself. It is okay to put your obedience to God first if He has given you an assignment. You know that God has a plan for your life and has promised you a new, better way of living. As a result, you're going to the next level, and you'll find that not everyone can go. In the next chapter, there are some hard decisions you will have to make. Are you ready to turn the page? It's time to shed the baggage that God has ordered you to leave behind.

Three Questions to Help You Assess Your Relationships

Cutting away and letting go of what God has already released from your life is difficult, but it saves heartache for you and offers others a season of lessons. Sometimes it's hard to know if someone should still be in your life as you journey to the destination God has for you. Are you still carrying along a person God has directed you to shed from your life? Here are some helpful questions to ask yourself as you evaluate your relationships.

Question #1: Does that person add value to your life?

I know it's a difficult question to answer because we want to be nice to everyone and make sure everyone is cared for and appreciated, but choosing not to take someone with you where God is elevating you doesn't make you a bad person. It just means that you would rather obey God than please man (Acts 5:29).

God had to give the prophet Samuel a stern warning after God took His anointing from King Saul. God asked Samuel, "How long will you mourn for Saul, seeing I have rejected him from reigning over Israel?" (1 Samuel 16:1 NKJV). Saul no longer added value to the kingdom of Israel, and God dethroned him. Perhaps you, like Samuel, need to move on.

Who is encouraging you and helping you in your season? Take another look inward. Do you give encouragement to the people who are adding value to your life? Strengthen those bonds and let the others go.

Question #2: Are you the only one giving?

In the relationship, are you the only one being flexible? Are you the only one pouring into the relationship? In this next season of your life, you must be careful of leeches.

Sometimes God brings acquaintances into your life that you make closer than you should. Sometimes you don't change location when God tells you to move, or you make something permanent that God means to be temporary. God directs people and things into your life, some for a season and some for a lifetime. Pray for the discernment to distinguish between the two.

As you progress through your seasons, ask yourself whether a relationship has passed its expiration date. What God instructs you to cut off will not fit where you are going. This is why Abram and Lot were experiencing tension in Genesis 13. Lot wasn't supposed to go with Abram through the new season.

Question #3: Is the mess in someone else's life causing you stress?

Most of the stress we deal with is a result of trying to resolve madness in someone else's life. Genesis 14 is an excellent example. Lot chose the land that appealed to his eyes, and others wanted it as well. Once war broke out, Lot and his family were taken captive. When Abram received word that his relatives had been captured, was he able to forget them? No, he wasn't. Abram took his own men and placed his own resources in jeopardy to go and save someone who should not have been with him in the first place.

Look at all of the messes you need to fix in your life. Are you bailing out people who should know better? Are you taking on the consequences meant for them?

When you are raising your children, you spend time cleaning up their messes, but you're actively teaching them to clean for themselves. When they're older, you can't keep bailing them out, time after time, keeping the hard consequences and lessons from their lives. Trust me, I know how hard this can be and the guilt you may experience from feeling like a bad parent and a bad friend. But it's not your place to act as God in their lives, instead of their own Heavenly Father. Just as when they were younger, if they make a mess, teach them how to clean it up. Then let them go. They need to be free and empowered to answer God's call on their own lives—and so do you.

A Destiny for You

Your destiny is at stake if you are spending too much time resolving issues that have nothing to do with you. Satan wants to keep you distracted by things that you cannot control. He wants you to stay focused on the wrong things so that you aren't fulfilling God's purpose for your life.

There's always someone in our lives that Satan uses to distract us. John 13:27 says, "As soon as Judas took the bread, Satan entered into him. So Jesus told him, 'What you are about to do, do quickly.'" Then Judas went about his treachery. Jesus knew what His purpose was on earth—to teach, to serve, and to save through His death. He also knew His own power to achieve those aims. Since Jesus knew what His destiny was, He told Judas to go about his work quickly.

You know that you have a destiny as well. God is calling you to a higher purpose, and He is calling you to leave behind those who hold you back. As hard as it may be, you need to shed the extra weight so you will be unencumbered as you move forward in God's will. Sometimes you have to set free your distractors into their destiny so that you can be free to walk into yours. Then your blessings can flow, as we will see in the next chapter.

WORKBOOK

Chapter Two Questions

Question: How did bringing Lot with him hinder and distract Abram from God's will? Describe a time when a close friend or family member kept you from fully surrendering to God and following His plan.

_____

_____

_____

_____

_____

_____

_____

_____

_____

_____

Question: What are some situations or relationships in which it would very rarely be God's will for you to separate from the other person, even if that person is not following God or encouraging you toward His plan for your life? What are some examples of one-sided relationships that are necessary in ministry or in obedience to God?

_____

_____

_____

_____

_____

_____

_____

_____

_____

_____

_____

Question: Is there a person God has told you to leave behind? What physical or emotional connections make it difficult to cut ties? How can you do so in a loving, gracious, yet decisive way?

_____

_____

_____

_____

_____

_____

_____

_____

_____

_____

_____

_____

Action: Study situations in the Bible when someone chose to step away from a relationship that was hindering God's work and will in his life. Was the separation natural or painful, temporary or permanent? What was the purpose of the separation, and (if known) what was the relationship like after the separation?

Examples: Samuel from King Saul (1 Samuel 15); David from Eliab (1 Samuel 17:28–30); Paul from John Mark and Barnabas (Acts 15:36–41; 2 Timothy 4:11); James and John from their father, Zebedee (Matthew 4:21–22); Jesus from His earthly family (Mark 3:31–35; John 7:1–10; John 19:25–27)

Chapter Two Notes

CHAPTER THREE

Your Blessing is on Schedule

In the 1994 box office hit *Forrest Gump*, the highly acclaimed actor Tom Hanks gave us this famous line: "My momma always said life was like a box of chocolates. You never know what you're gonna get."[2]

Even for Christians, life can seem random sometimes. Sudden changes can take us by surprise. Tragedy can seem to come out of nowhere. We can feel certain that we are heading in the right direction, only to come up against a dead end.

We know that God has a plan for us, but we can't see how it will play out. We don't always understand the purpose of everything we experience when it is happening. Not being able to see every step of the journey from the beginning can be frustrating. It makes us feel helpless. We may be tempted to believe that our lives are chaotic and out of control.

But God does not intend for His people to be helpless or hopeless. He is our help and our hope, and we have a personal line of communication with Him in the form of prayer. James 5:16b is a life-changing verse that says, "The prayer of a righteous person is powerful and effective."

Our prayers matter. When we are in our waiting season, we need to stay connected to God through prayer as well as Scripture study. Prayer and meditation will strengthen us spiritually to withstand the wait and also to receive what God has planned for us.

You can rely on the power of persistent prayer. When you request something of God that lines up with His will for you, your blessing is put on the schedule. It may not look exactly like what you expect, but it will be better than you ever dreamed. When you are waiting for God's answer, don't lose faith in His sovereignty, His goodness, His plan, and His purpose. What seems like a delay in the blessing God intends for you is actually His perfect timing.

Hannah's Blessing

One thing I love about God is how He gives hope in hopeless situations. Even in times when He seems to be ignoring our requests, He is actually preparing us for something greater than what we imagined.

Hannah was barren, meaning she could have no children, but God laid the desire on her heart to ask Him for a son (1 Samuel 1:2, 10–11). Her husband, Elkanah, a religious man, loved her and offered her extra kindness because God had not given her a child, while his other wife had many.

Year after year this man went up from his town to worship and sacrifice to the LORD Almighty at Shiloh, where Hophni and Phinehas, the two sons of Eli, were priests of the LORD. Whenever the day came for Elkanah to sacrifice, he would give portions of the meat to his wife Peninnah and to all her sons and daughters. But to Hannah he gave a double portion because he loved her, and the LORD had closed her womb.

—1 Samuel 1:3–5

Even though God was responsible for the delay in Hannah's blessings, He still showed her that He loved her and provided for her until the appointed time of her blessing.

Like Hannah, you may suffer heartache as you wait for God to answer the longing of your heart, but even in those difficult times, remember that He loves you. While you are going through your waiting season, God will give double portions of other kinds of care. God is so amazing that He can cause ravens to feed you in a drought, as He did for the prophet Elijah (1 Kings 17:1–6). The Israelites wandered in the desert for forty years due to their own disbelief and disobedience. During that time, God provided for them such that, as He reminded them, "your clothes and the sandals on your feet did not wear out" (Deuteronomy 29:5 HCSB). The prophet Jonah whined because he thought that God was too merciful to the repentant citizens of wicked Nineveh, but God still provided shade for Jonah from the sun (Jonah 4:1–6). God cares for us in our seasons of waiting, sometimes even in the waiting seasons that we bring upon ourselves.

Like Hannah, you may not be responsible for the

season you are in, but you are responsible for your actions in your barren seasons. Hannah must have hated the barren season. She wanted a son, but her complex emotions had to do with more than just wanting a son. Being barren in that time meant suffering the guilt, shame, and humiliation of not being able to produce a child for your husband. To make matters worse, tradition (not God) held that not being able to have a child meant you were cursed by God. Tradition also permitted a woman's husband to take another wife to give him children to carry on his name and legacy, though God never sanctioned this practice. Elkanah's other wife, Peninnah, had children, and she liked to rub it in:

> *Because the* Lord *had closed Hannah's womb, her rival kept provoking her in order to irritate her. This went on year after year. Whenever Hannah went up to the house of the* Lord, *her rival provoked her till she wept and would not eat. Her husband Elkanah would say to her, "Hannah, why are you weeping? Why don't you eat? Why are you downhearted? Don't I mean more to you than ten sons?"*
> *—1 Samuel 1:6–8*

How many of us would have given the other woman a piece of our minds? Hannah chose not to retaliate or give up hope. She turned faithfully to God through her difficult season of waiting:

> *Once when they had finished eating and drinking in Shiloh, Hannah stood up. Now Eli the priest was sitting on his chair by the doorpost of the* Lord's *house. In her deep anguish Hannah prayed to the* Lord, *weeping bitterly. And*

she made a vow, saying, "LORD Almighty, if you will only look on your servant's misery and remember me, and not forget your servant but give her a son, then I will give him to the LORD for all the days of his life, and no razor will ever be used on his head."

As she kept on praying to the LORD, Eli observed her mouth. Hannah was praying in her heart, and her lips were moving but her voice was not heard. Eli thought she was drunk and said to her, "How long are you going to stay drunk? Put away your wine."

"Not so, my lord," Hannah replied, "I am a woman who is deeply troubled. I have not been drinking wine or beer; I was pouring out my soul to the LORD. Do not take your servant for a wicked woman; I have been praying here out of my great anguish and grief."

—1 Samuel 1:9–16

When you really want something from God and your focus is on God, you don't give much attention to the small and insignificant. Sometimes we miss God and delay our blessings because we spend more time focusing on distractions. Hannah went every year with her husband to sacrifice to God, and her prayer was consistent.

God is a God of timing. He is strategic. He considers the big picture when working, and His vision is good and holy. His workings are so intricate that we cannot comprehend the full scope of them (Isaiah 55:8–9).

Hannah was praying for a son. God had already predestined that He needed a prophet for the nation of Israel to act on His behalf, but He would not birth the prophet before the predestined time or in Hannah's desired time. This blessing was on God's schedule.

Eli answered, "Go in peace, and may the God of Israel grant you what you have asked of him."

She said, "May your servant find favor in your eyes." Then she went her way and ate something, and her face was no longer downcast.
                                                           —1 Samuel 1:17–18

After that encounter with Eli, Hannah returned home. She became pregnant and gave birth to a son, Samuel, whom she offered to God and the temple. Hannah prayed to God during her difficult season of waiting. She was faithful and did not give up hope. God wasn't punishing Hannah, ignoring her, or rejecting her. Her blessing may have seemed delayed or denied, but in truth, God had it perfectly timed to fulfill His plan.

Spiritual Growth

The thing you have been praying to God for is not late. God hadn't forgotten about Hannah, and He has not forgotten about you. It's not that God hasn't heard your consistent and persistent prayers; it's about timing. Everything God has for you is predetermined. He may not send the promise when you want Him to send it or in the way you expect, but He will bring it right on time. Life is truly like a box of chocolates. You never know what you'll get or when you'll get it, but God does know.

If God had given Hannah the baby prematurely, there would have been no prophet to anoint King Saul or to bring the message that God was appointing a new king, King David. Hannah would never have been recorded in the Bible as a significant part of God's salvific plan. We wouldn't be saying her name and learning from her life thousands of years later. Hannah had a part to play in God's plan for the Messiah. Her son Samuel was instrumental in unfolding God's will for the kingship of the Davidic line, from which Jesus would eventually come.

Hannah put the things of God, the spiritual, before the things of this world. When we neglect our spiritual development, two things happen. First, our perception becomes skewed, and we can't see the hand of God working in our lives. Second, we become so burdened by our stress and our worldly, self-centered perspective that we cannot fully embrace and enjoy all that God is giving us and intends for us.

In his sermon "Brave Waiting" (1877), the noted scholar and theologian Charles H. Spurgeon quoted Psalm 27:14, "Wait on the LORD; be of good courage, and He shall strengthen your heart…" (NKJV). Spurgeon encouraged believers to be led by the Holy Spirit and to have courage in our waiting. He warned us not to get tired of waiting and give in to the temptation to put our trust in our flesh.[3] If we choose to wait on God, there will be a blessing in the waiting. We read in Isaiah that "those who wait on the LORD shall renew their strength…" (Isaiah 40:31 NKJV).

While we are waiting, we need to rely on God and stay connected to Him through prayer. James wrote, "You do not have *because you do not ask God.* When you ask, you do not receive, because you ask with wrong motives, that you may spend what you get on your pleasures" (James 4:2–3, emphasis added). Did you know that persistent prayer has the power to cause God to lean in your direction at His appointed time? However, effective prayer requires being in tune with God's will and putting His desires first. For this perspective, you need spiritual growth.

If you want to pray effectively, you also need to believe in the results. That means having faith, "the substance of things hoped for, the evidence of things not seen" (Hebrews 11:1 NKJV). That kind of faith can move mountains (Matthew 17:20).

Even if your mountain doesn't move right away, that doesn't mean God isn't there or doesn't care. God "will never leave you nor forsake you" (Hebrews 13:5 NKJV). He is attempting to show you how to change your perspective in your barren season. You may think that you are not being productive or making progress, but God is making progress in you. You are growing, and God is preparing the way.

You may be begging God for a blessing that you're afraid may never come. It may seem that God isn't listening, but He is. You may not receive your blessing as soon as you ask for it, but that doesn't mean your blessing isn't coming. It may not come in this season or even in the next one. It may not look the way you expect. But you will be blessed. That's a promise from God.

A Broken Masterpiece

A five-year-old girl wanted to color with her granddaddy. She loved to color. She would lay out all of the perfect, unbroken crayons in rows so she could choose what color she wanted for her masterpiece. Her granddaddy made her day when he said, "Go and get the crayons and the coloring book."

The little girl ran to grab the crayons and coloring book. On her way back, she dropped the crayons and accidentally stepped on some of them and broke them. She looked down at the broken crayons and sobbed, "I'll never be able to use them now!"

Her grandfather dried her tears and told her that not everything in life was going to be perfect. Other people wouldn't care whether the materials were flawed, whether the crayons were broken or the paint tubes were crinkled; they would only care about the masterpiece.

The little girl had convinced herself that the crayons had to be perfect and unbroken to be used. Sometimes you will go through seasons when you feel that you are too broken for God to use, but if you focus on your faith and remember that all things work together for your good (Romans 8:28), God will prove to you that broken crayons can still make color. God can use broken people to create masterpieces.

Hannah was tortured by others and felt like her body was broken, yet she remained true to her calling to pray. She had faith in God even before she was pregnant. She was given hope by the priest, and she was no longer sad. When you choose to live by faith, your perception changes. You can learn how to shout joyfully to the Lord in a season of waiting because you know that your blessing is on the way. The joy that comes from faith is another color in the masterpiece. Be determined, as Hannah was determined, to continue in faith until you see the fulfillment of God's promise.

Determination in Season

Hannah's determination is remarkable and inspirational. She had the spirit of purpose, and she exercised her will regardless of her exterior circumstances. Although it was the custom of men to take only their children to worship at Shiloh, one of the three festivals they observed, the Bible says that Hannah went every year. Are you still able to worship when it seems like God is not answering your prayers? A persistent prayer life, like Hannah's, leads to the confident belief in God's timing.

Often our stress overcomes our determination. Many of us experience pressure from a desire to figure God out. How can we comprehend the mind of a God whose wisdom and knowledge are infinite? Wouldn't life be simpler and more enjoyable if we would stop trying to figure God out and start trusting His Word? When we're determined to figure God out, we're not looking for the right things. Instead, we need to be determined in prayer, as Hannah was.

Are All of Your Wants Bad?

A preschooler raised his hand and asked for a snack.

The teacher didn't draw back in shock and demand why the child would ask such a thing, threatening to tell the child's parents immediately, nor did she call the authorities on the child. Why?

There's nothing wrong with what the child asked for. In fact, a snack can be a good thing.

So, what did the teacher do? She glanced at the clock and saw that it was close to lunchtime. She knew that it was natural for the children to be hungry, but if they ate a snack now, it would spoil their lunch. The snack would have to wait until the middle of the day, and it would need to be a healthy snack.

Sometimes—a lot of times—we are like preschoolers who want a snack that we think looks good and satisfying, and we want it right away. But God, our Teacher, knows what's best for us. He knows exactly what we need, which is better than what we, with our limited vision, ask for. We need to trust God's timing and His choice.

Hannah's child would come at the perfect time. It wasn't wrong for Hannah to ask for a child, but she needed to wait on God's holy timing. Hannah's waiting season prepared her spiritually to offer the child to God and the temple.

Going through life, you may not understand how bad relationships, the loss of a job, or the loss of a loved one will work for your good. Hannah's example teaches us that we need to have faith, even when we can't see the purpose of our suffering. Faith means trusting God and taking Him at His Word. Even though you can't see His plan, you need to trust that it is in motion.

The only way to stay faithful through a waiting season is to stay in contact with God through His Word, prayer, and worship. Don't worry about trying to figure out what God is doing. That's not your job. Trust that God knows best and allow Him to use you as He sees fit. Like Hannah, you no longer have to feel sad in your time of waiting. Instead, cling to God's promises and rejoice in the knowledge that He is preparing you for what's ahead.

God gives purpose in waiting. Your season of becoming is when you find God and draw closer to Him. Only He can weave together the broken pieces of your life into the new person He wants you to be.

WORKBOOK

Chapter Three Questions

Question: What have been some surprises, good or bad, that have made your life different from what you imagined it would be?

_____

_____

_____

_____

_____

_____

_____

_____

_____

_____

Question: What are some ways you have seen a double portion of God's care during a season of waiting, whether that season was brought on by your own mistakes or by God's sovereign timing?

_____

_____

_____

_____

_____

_____

_____

_____

_____

_____

_____

Question: List the attitudes that characterized Hannah's heart and actions as she waited on the Lord for her heart's desire. Do these same attitudes characterize you as you wait on the Lord? In what ways could you be more like Hannah?

_____

_____

_____

_____

_____

_____

_____

_____

_____

_____

_____

_____

_____

Action: God's perfect timing is easier to see in retrospect. For each example below, consider how God's timing was better than man's timing. What happened in the person's life and/or outward circumstances during the waiting period?

- Joseph dreamed of being a great ruler at age 17, and he became second-in-command in Egypt at age 30.

- Moses wanted to deliver his people, but he messed it up. He spent the next four decades as a shepherd in the wilderness before God called him to return to Egypt.

- Caleb was ready to take the promised land at age 40, but he had to wait forty-five years to claim his inheritance because of the faithlessness of the rest of his generation.

- David was anointed king over Israel as a teen, but he wasn't crowned king until the age of 30.

- Jesus was ready to begin ministry at age 12, but He went back to Nazareth with His parents and waited until He was about 30 to begin His mission.

Chapter Three Notes

_____

_____

_____

_____

_____

_____

_____

_____

_____

_____

_____

_____

_____

_____

_____

_____

_____

_____

_____

_____

_____

CHAPTER FOUR

The Characteristics of a New Man

There was a time when I wanted to impress others. I wanted people to look at me and think that I was somebody, that I was important and good-looking. I wanted respect. I thought that dressing the part, trying a new mustache, shaving my head just right, or flashing the perfect smile was what I should focus on. Clothes made the man, or so I thought.

My image was so important to me that I took money from my grocery budget to purchase the right outfit. Let me rephrase: There was a time when I would rather starve than go without a fancy suit.

Hear me clearly when I tell you that having your priorities out of order can cost you big time. I can still recall the morning when my shoes almost caused me to miss my flight to San Francisco. I woke up late and had to rush to get dressed. I had already mentally planned the perfect pair of shoes to match my travel outfit, but when I looked for them, I couldn't find them. Instead of simply choosing another pair, I just had to search for those shoes.

By the time I found them, I was thirty minutes behind schedule. When I got to the airport, I had to empty my suitcase to fit clothes in another bag because I had packed too much stuff. I was really running late. Was everything smooth sailing from there? Of course not. There was a delay in the screening process because I had to take off my high-top sneakers—the very shoes I had made myself late trying to find in the first place. I almost missed my plane for the sake of those shoes. My priorities were seriously out of whack.

Today I am a new man, and while I often wear a suit, my motivation is to dress nicely for God because I respect Him. Why prioritize impressing others, who may not even really care about us, over living in a way that is pleasing to God? With increased confidence in the Lord, we understand that we no longer have to go into debt to impress people.

Why the change of heart? When we become new in Christ, our mindset must change:

> *Since, then, you have been raised with Christ, set your hearts on things above, where Christ is, seated at the right hand of God. Set your minds on things above, not on earthly things. For you died, and your life is now hidden with Christ in God. When Christ, who is your life, appears, then you also will appear with him in glory.*
> **—Colossians 3:1–4**

When our mindset changes, our priorities change. We put more emphasis on the inner person than the outer image. Some of the challenges we face are struggles against the old nature still fighting for control within us. We need to stop worrying so much about material things and concern ourselves more with clothing ourselves in godly character:

> *Therefore, as God's chosen people, holy and dearly loved, clothe yourselves with compassion, kindness, humility, gentleness and patience.*
> **—Colossians 3:12**

I could wear the fanciest suit to try to earn respect, but if I'm not compassionate, kind, humble, gentle, and patient, I am living apart from God's will for my life.

Your Position and Condition in Christ

There's a difference between your *position* in Christ and your *condition* in Christ. Once you are saved, your position is solidified. Jesus said, "My Father, who has given them to Me, is greater than all; and no one is able to snatch them out of My Father's hand" (John 10:29 NKJV). You are a child of God, and your future with Him is ensured.

You're not living in a time without God anymore. Your entire old self was cast aside when you believed and were baptized (Ephesians 4:22–24). Your position in Christ has changed once for all. No one can take you away from Him. You can look at life with the power of victory because the old was buried and the new was raised with Christ (Romans 6:3–11).

However, your condition in Christ can change when you sin and "fall short of the glory of God" (Romans 3:23). Sin's consequences can separate us from God and even cause death (Romans 6:23), but that death does not keep believers from heaven. Sin damages our relationship with God but does not change our position with Him. As God's children, we are "co-heirs with Christ" (Romans 8:14–17). We have keys and access to the Kingdom, and we can act in authority as children of the King (Matthew 16:19). That doesn't mean we should do whatever we want. Our sins hurt God. He takes it personally when we choose to disobey Him. As believers, we have an assured future, but we can be distant from our Father if we sin.

Your *position* is unchangeable and comes with some powerful benefits. First of all, you are saved, and that cannot change. You belong to God forever. Not even Satan can take you from His hand.

Not only that, but you can also experience God's power in your life right now. You can speak into a situation and witness God's power in action. You are not limited or defeated when you are acting in Jesus' name. This access to God's power in any situation should give you confidence to proclaim Him anytime and in any place. As you develop spiritually, you will see this power grow.

God has your back. He will protect you and deal with your enemies. You are the King's kid. You can say to your enemies, "I'm not going to do the fighting. If you want to get to me, you have to go through my Dad first!"

Your *condition*, on the other hand, depends on you. If you choose to allow sin to direct your life after salvation, your sinful actions will push you further from God and rob you of joy. You will not experience the fullness of blessing that God intends for you in your life on earth.

Instead, choose to live as a person who has been saved. Choose to please God by following His will. Allow the new perspective He gives you to transform your life from the inside out. When you are a new man, you know that God is in control. You defer decisions, your personal and spiritual growth, and your emotional health to Him.

When you surrender to God's sovereignty, you leave room for Him to work in people and situations. You know that you don't need to worry. God's got this. This view leads to increasing joy as, time after time, you see evidence of God taking control.

Being in a good condition before God requires spending time in prayer and reading His Word. These activities bring you closer to God, which will develop specific godly characteristics in you.

Key Characteristics of a New Man

Colossians 3:1 says, "Since, then, you have been raised with Christ, set your hearts on things above, where Christ is, seated at the right hand of God." Where is your heart? What do you love? Have you fallen in love with things that please your flesh but bring no glory to God? If you set your heart on Christ, you will save yourself some headaches and heartaches. If you love your home, your car, your job, or your hobby, you're destined for some bad seasons. It's okay to enjoy those things, but where's your heart? How devastated would you be if those things were taken away?

The first word of the verse, "since," takes out the excuses. "Since" means that you are raised in Christ, no question. No one is taking that away. But when something bad happens, depending on where your heart is, you might feel like life is over.

Because of your position, you have the power to change your condition by setting your heart on things above. Too many of us focus on earthly things rather than on God. Jesus said, "But seek first his kingdom and his righteousness, and all these things will be given to you as well" (Matthew 6:33). God doesn't want you to seek houses or clothes or groceries. He will provide for all of your needs. God will change what you desire when you change your outlook and place your focus on Him.

The more you learn about Christ, the more you will develop the characteristics of a new man. When you're in a season of becoming, in a holding pattern, it's because your attitude needs to catch up with what God wants to do in your life.

It's like you have a new house gifted to you, and you ring the doorbell, not realizing that the keys are in your pocket. You already have access. The essential characteristic of a new man is that he continually taps into his access to Christ. When there's trouble, he turns to God first. It's a natural and holy response. You are in a season of becoming so that you can learn to turn to God in all things.

Keeping Your Eyes on Him

Now that you know your position and condition, set your mind on things above. Are you looking up, or are you looking down beneath your feet? Could it be that the reason you are so stressed out is because you are too concerned with the things beneath you? Gossip, backbiting, and lying are all under your feet. Look up and let the Lord fight your battles.

Since you are now on God's team, you don't need to disobey Him. Disobedience doesn't look pretty.

> *Put to death, therefore, whatever belongs to your earthly nature: sexual immorality, impurity, lust, evil desires and greed, which is idolatry. Because of these, the wrath of God is coming. You used to walk in these ways, in the life you once lived. But now you must also rid yourselves of all such things as these: anger, rage, malice, slander, and filthy language from your lips. Do not lie to each other, since you have taken off your old self with its practices and have put on the new self, which is being renewed in knowledge in the image of its Creator.*
> *—Colossians 3:5–10*

Who sins? Everyone, "for all have sinned and fall short of the glory of God" (Romans 3:23). God hates sin, and sinful behavior will keep a believer from living in close relationship with God. People consumed by anger and wrath will never be able to experience the pinnacle of Christian living in every area of their lives. Their unwillingness to forgive shows that they don't truly understand and receive God's forgiveness of them and Christ's sacrificial work on the cross.

Those given over to malice and slander are likely to talk about other people in a negative sense. They may use filthy language, which is typically a byproduct of anger.

Lying is a behavior that's in direct opposition to "the God of truth" (Isaiah 65:16 NKJV), whose "word is truth" (John 17:17). It does you no harm to tell the truth unless you're embarrassed about what you're doing. We are still held accountable before God for "little" lies.

When you keep your eyes on Christ, these sins aren't appealing anymore. The more time you spend with Him, the less you sin. Feeding the spirit instead of the flesh is about staying close to God and not loving the things of this world. Sin feels good to the flesh, but now that you belong to God, you need to put on the characteristics of a new man. Are you willing to do the hard work to feed the spirit inside of you? Thank God for His transformative power!

When your heart is fixed on God instead of on the things of the earth, you'll be able to stop focusing on how you've been wronged and hurt. You won't be focusing on how long and painful your waiting season seems. Instead, you will be growing spiritually and looking for how God can use you in your circumstances.

Feeding the spirit instead of the flesh means transforming the way you relate to others. Don't buy a big house or a fancy car to impress people. Put on compassion, kindness, gentleness, and humility. Put on patience, love, and thankfulness. Put on the words of Christ. We can't win the spiritual fight without the Word in us for every situation we face.

Give God the praise. Take off your old self and walk in your newness. Then the season you are in will become refreshing, and you will emerge powerful in your destiny.

WORKBOOK

Chapter Four Questions

Question: Contrast your human efforts at creating a new image with God's supernatural gift of a new identity in Christ. Which one is your primary focus?

_____

_____

_____

_____

_____

_____

_____

_____

_____

_____

_____

Question: In your own words, describe your *position* in Christ and your *condition* in Him. How does God use seasons of waiting to work on your condition?

_____

_____

_____

_____

_____

_____

_____

_____

_____

_____

Question: What are some practical ways you can draw close to God and feed the spirit rather than the flesh?

_____

_____

_____

_____

_____

_____

_____

_____

_____

_____

_____

_____

Action: Looking to God to see how He can use you shortens your wait. Pray about and contemplate how God can use you right now in your season of waiting. Whom can you encourage, disciple, or serve? How can you share the gospel with others? What skills, gifts, and abilities can you begin or continue developing that God may use for His glory in your next season? Pick something practical you can do this week to make yourself more available to be used by God.

Chapter Four Notes

_____

_____

_____

_____

_____

_____

_____

_____

_____

_____

_____

_____

_____

_____

_____

_____

_____

_____

_____

_____

_____

_____

_____

CHAPTER FIVE

Keeping Your Eye on the Prize

You may be called to wait, but you're not meant to wait passively. Abraham grew rich while he waited. He was working to better himself and his holdings (Genesis 13:2). He had a goal.

Imagine a pilot about to take off who is twiddling his thumbs or idly checking his phone. When he gets a call from the tower that it's his turn to take off, he thunders into the air, only to realize that he's not sure where to go. He didn't work the flight plan.

The pilot needs a destination, a goal for the flight. Otherwise he'll jam up runways across America as everyone waits for him to figure out what he's doing.

Similarly, as Christians, we must use our seasons of becoming to prepare to obey God's plan. It helps to know what we're waiting for. Without knowing the goal, we don't know when we've reached the end of our waiting.

Pretend that you're being called to save money for a trip, but you don't know the destination or how much it will cost. You might save up money your entire life and never know where to go. However, if you know that the trip is to Hawaii, you know exactly how much to save, when to stop saving, and when to book your flights and hotels. With that in mind, we need to seek God for direction. When we know where He is leading us, we can better prepare for our calling.

Sometimes it's easy to articulate the goal, such as a particular lifestyle change or a specific sin issue you want to address. Other times, the goal may be more ambiguous. Perhaps you want to grow closer to the Lord. Maybe you're depressed or anxious and you long for freedom from the overwhelming emotional burden. If you're feeling aimless, seek God to reveal the goals He has for you.

The Right Kind of Goal

Remember that no matter how long your waiting season is, it's not meant to be your final destination. Philippians 1:6 encourages us to be "confident of this, that he who began a good work in you will carry it on to completion until the day of Christ Jesus." It isn't over until God says it's over. He hasn't finished working in you yet, so don't get too comfortable in your waiting season! You are meant to be growing and preparing for your next season.

However, you need to be careful that the goals you set are about God's business, not worldly things. Too many people of God focus on the wrong things, and they end up disappointed, frustrated, and unsatisfied. As we discussed previously, you need to keep your eyes on Christ and concern yourself with "things above" (Colossians 3:1–2). Your goals will come from setting your heart on God. His goals will become your goals.

One useful way to tell if you're focused on pleasing God or the flesh is to see if your praise is predicated on the situation or if you're simply praising God. Ask yourself, "Is this about me, or is this about God?" If you are putting "confidence in the flesh" (Philippians 3:3) and pursuing goals for the sake of your own glory or a sense of worldly stability, validation, and justification, then you and God are not on the same page.

Talents Versus Gifts

The goals you set should take into consideration your natural talents and gifts from the Holy Spirit. Natural talents are the types of things you tend to be good at doing, such as singing or mathematics. Giftings from the Spirit are gifts given to you supernaturally by God's Spirit for the glorification of God and the edification of the body of Christ. You would not have these gifts without the empowerment of the Holy Spirit (1 Corinthians 12). Just about everybody has at least one natural talent, but only believers have gifts from the Holy Spirit.

Satan tries to trick us into perfecting our natural talents while neglecting the gifts of the Spirit. The truth is that all good things are from God (James 1:17). All good things are to be developed and offered for the glory of God and the building up of the body of Christ, as well as the personal growth of the believer.

God wants you to use all of the gifts He gives you, both

spiritual and natural, in the time and way He instructs. Don't merely trust in your natural talents for success; trust in Jesus and His Spirit at work in you. Don't just coast through life with your talents; stretch yourself in the anointing of your gifts. God intends to grow you, not make you comfortable. Make sure that you come out of your waiting season ready to fulfill God's call upon your life.

Support for Your Goals

Once God has revealed the right goal for you to pursue, the next step is to find support for your goal. Be careful not to hang around people who will encourage you to buy into your own hype or put confidence in the flesh. Your confidence needs to be in Christ. Paul wrote:

> *What is more, I consider everything a loss because of the surpassing worth of knowing Christ Jesus my Lord, for whose sake I have lost all things. I consider them garbage, that I may gain Christ and be found in him, not having a righteousness of my own that comes from the law, but that which is through faith in Christ—the righteousness that comes from God on the basis of faith.*
> —**Philippians 3:8–9**

There may still be people who try to convince you to do certain things to earn salvation. As Paul asked the Galatians, "Who has bewitched you?" (Galatians 3:1). Believing that Christ died for you is enough. It is imperative to put your faith and trust in God alone, not in your own talents and not in people who will feed you lies contrary to God's Word. Relying on the wrong person for support can leave you empty and in serious trouble regarding your future.

To move to the next level and get ready for your next season, you need to change your focus. Your motivation and ultimate goal should be to know and please Christ. There is nobody greater, so you need to look to Him, first and foremost, for direction and support. Then all of the pieces of your life will fall into place. God will give you the desire of your heart if you decide to put your trust in Him. If He can raise the dead, He can certainly lead you to your destination and provide all of the resources you need along the way.

Strip the negative support. You can't carry the weight of extra baggage where God is leading you, so leave it behind. This might involve deleting Facebook friends and phone numbers to remove toxic influences from your life. Knowing Christ is more important than anything else, so let go of everything that gets in the way of that goal.

Confidence in Moving Ahead

Rejoice in the Lord! You have a gift from God. You have the opportunity not only to know Him personally, but also to contribute to His will. However, many of us want to rejoice only when life is easy and things are going well. When Paul wrote in Philippians 3:8, "I consider everything a loss because of the surpassing worth of knowing Christ Jesus my Lord," he was writing to a group of people who were in danger of putting their confidence in their flesh. We're the same. If we're going to reach our destination, we must first learn to rejoice in the Lord even when it seems like our blessing is a long time coming.

Confidence that we are making forward progress comes from knowing that our God is worthy of praise. We cannot look to our circumstances to make us happy or give us confidence. Instead, we must look to the goodness of the Lord and rejoice!

> *I rejoiced greatly in the Lord that at last you renewed your concern for me. Indeed, you were concerned, but you had no opportunity to show it. I am not saying this because I am in need, for I have learned to be content whatever the circumstances. I know what it is to be in need, and I know what it is to have plenty. I have learned the secret of being content in any and every situation, whether well fed or hungry, whether living in plenty or in want. I can do all this through him who gives me strength.*
> **—Philippians 4:10–13**

Paul was in a Roman jail cell when he wrote, "Rejoice in the Lord always. I will say it again: Rejoice!" (Philippians 4:4). You can live with joy in any situation when your joy comes from knowing Christ.

Being joyful and content in any situation doesn't mean that you are meant to stay where you are forever. Paul also wrote, "But one thing I do: Forgetting what is behind and straining toward what is ahead, I press on toward the goal to win the prize for which God has called me heavenward in Christ Jesus" (Philippians 3:13b–14).

As you press on, forget what's behind. Forgetting is the process of accidentally or deliberately failing to remember people or ideas. You can't travel into the next season with all of the baggage you're carrying now. Are you still connected to people who try to pull you away from your God? Cut those ties. Are you still stressing over a job you lost two years ago? God took it from you because you didn't have the courage to leave it behind. Are you still mad at your ex? Let go of your anger. Where is holding on to the past going to get you?

Keep straining forward to what is ahead. As you reach for the goal, you will always be stretched. It's not supposed to be easy or comfortable. It's supposed to make you grow.

Strive energetically for the fulfillment of your purpose in Christ. You won't reach your destiny by accident, and you won't reach it by your own strength. You must submit to God's plan for your future and be obedient to the steps He leads you to take. The prize He has for you is beyond anything you could ever dream up for yourself. It is well worth the wait.

Chapter Five Questions

Question: What are your goals? What are you waiting for, hoping for, and working for in your life? Can you truly say that knowing Christ is your most important goal? What might you be prioritizing over Him?

_____

_____

_____

_____

_____

_____

_____

_____

_____

Question: What are your talents? Are you using them to promote yourself or to glorify God? How can you tell the difference?

_____

_____

_____

_____

_____

_____

_____

_____

_____

_____

_____

Question: What are your spiritual gifts? How are you developing them and using them to glorify God and build up His church?

_____

_____

_____

_____

_____

_____

_____

_____

_____

_____

_____

_____

Action: Write out a prayer committing your waiting time to God and His plan for you. Decide how you will start using this time to serve and learn, rather than wasting it on worldly distractions.

Chapter Five Notes

CONCLUSION

You're in Good Hands

These days, I take far more care when packing for trips. I know that the journey is far, and I don't want to carry heavy bags or pay extra to bring clothes I'm not going to wear.

I lay out a single suitcase and think through the trip. What are my goals? What will help me succeed? I pack only what is needed, and if there's anything extra in the bag that doesn't work, I leave it behind without regret.

There's a long wait at the airport, but I don't get stressed about it. I know that this time of preparation before departure is for my own safety. Sometimes I chat with others as we wait. Other times, I read a book or simply enjoy a cup of coffee.

Once I'm on the plane, I study or review for my upcoming assignment or engage in conversations with the other passengers. I know that the pilot has checked the plane for safety and prepped for the flight plan. There's no need to worry. I'm in good hands.

There's a problem on the runway, so we have to circle the city for a few moments before we land. I close my eyes and rest.

I know that God is the master pilot of my life. He knows when it's the perfect time to approach the landing strip. God will not allow you to reach your destination in a season when you are not prepared to handle where He is taking you. The delay is not punishment; it's preparation.

God is in charge. Your job is to shed the weight He instructs you to shed. God will strip away from you anything you put in His place. The blessing in shedding the extra weight is that when you reach the destination He has planned for you, you will be able to enjoy it to the fullest.

You don't have to wait for your destination to live with joy. You can enjoy your waiting season. It doesn't have to be a time of frustration and stagnation. God means for it to be a season of spiritual growth and preparation. God wants to use your season of becoming to teach you about Himself and to help you learn to rely on Him.

If you seek God in His Word and in prayer, He will direct your steps. Drawing closer to God will change your priorities. You will want to glorify Him and please Him. His desires will become your desires. You will learn who He wants you to be.

As your spiritual life strengthens, your picture of God's character will become clearer. You will gain personal experience of His goodness, His love, and His power. Then you will be able to take on seasons of waiting, seasons of action, seasons of trial, and seasons of blessing with confidence because you know that you can trust your God.

May He grant you peace and joy in all of your seasons

and bring you into the fullness of who He created you to be.

REFERENCES

Notes

1. Easton, M. G. "Abram." *Illustrated Bible Dictionary*. 3rd ed. Thomas Nelson, 1897.

2. Zemeckis, Robert. *Forrest Gump*. Paramount Pictures. 1994.

3. Spurgeon, Charles Haddon. "Brave Waiting." August 26, 1877. In *Metropolitan Tabernacle Pulpit* (vol. 23). In *The Spurgeon Center for Biblical Preaching at Midwestern Seminary*. https://www.spurgeon.org/resource-library/sermons/brave-waiting#flipbook/.

About the Author

Pastor Erick W. Hoskin Sr. is the senior pastor and founder of the **Word of God Christian Fellowship Church** in Cypress, Texas, where he is known for his heart, humor, and clear presentation of the gospel. Since its launch in 2010, the Word Church of Cypress, as it is known colloquially, has grown from eight members in Pastor Hoskin's home to over eight hundred members and two Sunday services.

Pastor E is the Son of Dr. Willie (*Superintendent of the Natchez Public School System*) and Lillie (*Principal*) Hoskin. He hails from Natchez, Mississippi, and is a graduate of Natchez Adams

High School. He furthered his education at Alcorn State University, where he earned a Bachelor of Science in Business Administration. In addition to his B.S. in Administration, Pastor Hoskin holds a theological studies degree (2013) as well as a Master of Biblical Studies (2015) from Grace School of Theology. He is also preparing to pursue his MDiv in the fall of 2019.

Pastor E has long possessed an interest in empowering and inspiring people at an early age. He accepted his call to preach the gospel under the guidance of Pastor John B. Hollmon. After being licensed to preach by Pastor Hollmon, Pastor E went on to leadership roles in various ministries at the Fellowship of Redeeming Truth Church (FORT). Serving as assistant pastor at the FORT, he provided leadership to the youth ministry, marriage ministry, and men's ministry.

Before birthing the Word Church of Cypress, Pastor E preached the gospel of Jesus Christ in churches, conventions, conferences, and revivals throughout the United States. He is the founder of the Word of God Christian Fellowship's Real Men Standing UP (RMSU) ministry. He is also the founder of E.W.H. Ministries (*"Ministry that reaches outside the four walls of the church"*), which affords him the opportunity to host empowerment conferences throughout the states of Texas, Mississippi, and Louisiana. This ministry is known for its charity and community involvement (e.g., providing scholarships and hosting a father/daughter dance, golf tournaments, and gospel brunches).

He is active in the local Cypress community, where he serves as a member of the Community Leadership Coalition (CLC) with the Cypress Fairbanks Independent School District. Pastor E also served on the 2014 CFISD Long Term Planning Committee and is a member of the Cy-Fair Chamber of Commerce.

To God be the glory—in eight years' time, Pastor E led the church in acquiring and dedicating a multi-million-dollar project (an 11,000 sq. ft. worship edifice, built on seven acres of land at 17902 Telge Road, Cypress, TX 77429). Weekly live broadcasts of both services, social media, and an interactive website now connect the world to the Word of God family. (Learn more about Word of God Christian Fellowship at www.wogcf.org.)

Pastor E's ultimate desire for WOGCF is to see Christ exalted, disciples made, and believers equipped for gospel proclamation. It is his desire to carry the proclaimed gospel of Jesus Christ with power, anointing, revelation and edification.

About Sermon To Book

SermonToBook.com began with a simple belief: that sermons should be touching lives, *not* collecting dust. That's why we turn sermons into high-quality books that are accessible to people all over the globe.

Turning your sermon series into a book exposes more people to God's Word, better equips you for counseling, accelerates future sermon prep, adds credibility to your ministry, and even helps make ends meet during tight times.

John 21:25 tells us that the world itself couldn't contain the books that would be written about the work of Jesus Christ. Our mission is to try anyway. Because in heaven, there will no longer be a need for sermons or books. Our time is now.

If God so leads you, we'd love to work with you on your sermon or sermon series.

Visit www.sermontobook.com to learn more.

Made in the USA
Middletown, DE
16 January 2022

58784405R10056